CW00434168

Barefoot Like The Earth

by Dakota Wint

Barefoot Like The Earth was written between the years 2012-2022,
which was the unusual decade of my 20s.

This collection of poetry highlights the heartache of being young,
it reveals my challenges in self-discovery,
my experiences traveling the world,
my search for a tangible spirituality,
and my overall journey coping with the strangeness of being alive.

Most of the words you will read come from the cold basement
of my family house in Detroit,
or from scribbled notes on long bus rides
in the Himalayan mountains of India,
from vision-dazed jungle huts in the Amazon,
or from the mystical carpet-draped alleyways of the Middle East –

I never expected my feet to take me where they have taken me,
but I've found inspiration and poetry
in the streets that I've stumbled down.

I hope to share some of my journey and thoughts with you.

"Sometimes words just want to be alive
for the sake of whoever needs to hear them."
-Dakota Wint

Dedications

When acknowledging the beautiful strangeness
of being alive in this universe,
poetry arises naturally and spontaneously.

I believe this recognition of strangeness
is the basis of all art, religion, and philosophy;
in some ways, I feel even love is a reflection of this recognition.

When you're in love, in any form,
the moment seems to carry actual weight.
It's measurable compared to the moments
you're unaligned or feeling lonely.

So, to my lovers throughout time,
my family, my friends,
and those who have dared me to look inside myself
to seek something more from life.

You have all inspired me to undoubtedly feel
as if something divine is taking place within every heart
and in the illumination of every eye.

Thanks for helping me see.

Enjoy this book.

Yours,
D.W.

(Dakota Wint at Giza plateau in Cairo, Egypt October 31st, 2017)

Poems by page

The following poems were written between 2012-2022.
They are not arranged in chronological order.

Mount Somewhere

Watery eyes
from the top of Mount Somewhere

I'm not sure if I'm crying
or if the wind is just happy to see me

I wipe my nose along a sleeve of cotton trees
I nudge myself close to the ledge
and close my eyes

I won't say a word cause there isn't any

If only I knew all that's happened where I stood,
i'd fall to my knees

I hold a leaf in my hand;
this place is the holy land.
I see now,
all places are the holy land.

I have nowhere to be,
so I'll go everywhere

Like the soul hitch-hikes
through the body of all lives

Mount Somewhere

Is the world just churches and jails?

A bruise punched into a twilight sky
by the fist of an Old Testament God

I'm watching the wind blow patterns on a field
and I put my hands in the dirt

I've never been to Nepal
but there's this patch on my bag
stitched on by some thrift shop ghost
that my dirty clothes now haunt

He must have looked at the same sky I see

There will come a day when you realize
everything goes
and it'll be bitter

But life will finally have meaning.

At least the world is not as lonely
as I make it out to be.

Parvati Valley, India
2019

Guidance

I ask the blackness of the sky for guidance
Even though I already know

To close a chapter is hard
But necessary

To know sacrifice

Do not clutch when it's time to move on

Sometimes waves of sadness just hit me
and idk why
because i don't really have anything
to be sad about

2022

Lacadon forest

I took a wooden boat across the river
into Guatemala
illegally

Everyone is looking at me confused
I bought a Gatorade and left

Time doesn't care how great you will become.
It doesn't care about anything, actually,
other than going somewhere,
and honestly, I don't either.

Do what ya can
cause getting old just means more bad news.

I can't believe there's WiFi this deep in the jungle.
The Lacandon woman charges me
$1.25 per hour of internet that I use.

We've manifested a Technological Earth
through our rituals of work
and our worship of products.

I know it seems counter intuitive
but I feel like this is the way it's supposed to be,
despite the state of things.

Lacacdon forest

Josué took me into the selva.
You can't step through here without tripping on
undiscovered ruins.
He calls it the lost city of Lacanja.

We just keep walking.

We get to an old temple on a hill
Trees grow from the roof
Proving nature is the real religion

Josué pulls out a joint
from a bag made of twisted rope

Now we are friends from different places
and we are high
in the ancestral afterworld

The Lost City of Lacanja, Chiapas
October 15 2020

Earthdream

I wonder,
Who are the people in my dreams?
Am I the people in my dreams
And is the floor me, too?

Why would this world be any different?
The world above is the world below
and it all fades
into something else
eventually.

Dreams are not shrug-worthy happenings
and life is not a shrug-worthy happening

We live in so many places at once
and eventually,
we forget them all

From the wakefulness of life,
to the flash of a dream,
to the blackness of sleep
We surrender our authority
to the temporarily arising reality
that we find ourselves bewildered
by in this moment

Earthdream

But look closely
There is one unchanging constant
through which you flow eternally

It watches from the background.

Who is being carried through this flow?

What you're looking for is what's looking.

Who can say what this life is?

Maybe it is not something to be said
but felt

All of it is you
and you have no idea

January 2020

Earth is alive, magic is real

I had a dream that hundreds of coyotes
burned down my house last night
The entire sky was covered in smoke

It always feels like time
is leading up to something

but it just keeps

go
i
n

g

Earth is alive, magic is real

She took a hit from a joint
that she had covered
by the side of her hair

and she said,
"I believe if two people are sincere enough,
they can find each other in the afterlife."

I smile and nod
because she doesn't realize
that's what's happening

She wouldn't pass it.
Red eye'd babe,
you're not who you think you are.

The Earth is alive
and magic
is
real

Libertad, Peru
Feb. 2020

Ayahuasca

The Bruja sings
as I drink her soup

My stomach becomes a swamp of snakes
Vines wrap my lungs
and there are bugs inside my throat

The Genie of the jungle
is a dancing Medusa inside my head

I am stoned inside of a plants dream

Curandera, sing your song
carry me through your world of 25,000 colors

I am not my body
and my source of pride is shame

Ancient ancestors stepped their way into my feet.

I watch the same moon reflect onto ancient water.

Ayahuasca

I am a child of the prehistoric echo.

In the beginning, was the word
and I am here to say,

"I love you."

This place moves so fast.
It feels solid.

Vibrations turned to visions.

Chaikuni crossroad point me on the way
Flying eagle man and his pink flower.

Big teeth,
mud monsters,
dead girls,
praying mantis,
cosmic operation table
rainbow doctors, and
strange healers

There is a world of spirits

inside the plants.

Notes after Shipibo Ceremony
Ucayali, Peru
January 2020

For whatever strangeness

Grab a pen and paper
and start writing

Scribble something so true
That whoever reads it has no choice but to believe you

Say something that'll make us all shut up for once
Say something that'll make us remember
the ground beneath our feet is more alive than us

'Cause, when we're dead and gone,
this dirt will be the only thing echoing our story
through the nutrients
our bodies give the Earth

In the end, you won't remember
the time you spent yawning
or tapping your foot

so be true and vulnerable
and say what you mean

Because for whatever strangeness,

you've taken birth.

2019

Velada in Oaxaca

Mountain top medicine woman
with a handful of saints
7 yellow candles
and copal for the night
Mother Mary's here too
with the spirit of Earth
I'm taking deep breaths in
just to be sure

The walls are speaking
and colors alive

A still and quiet boy
with kaleidoscope eyes

After a Mazatecan Mushroom Ceremony
Huatula De Jiménez Oaxaca, Mexico
April 2019

The easy way

You can tell everything you need to know
about a person
if you look them in the eyes
and even see the whole universe
if you stare deep enough.

To avoid any sign of self reflection,
most of us walk through life
with our heads toward the ground.

We take the easy way.

I guess there's nothing wrong with that.

The easy way is easy

but the long way holds mystery
and something else

The easy way

Haven't you ever looked at the line
that separates the sky from the Earth
and just wanted to start walking?

What's going on over there?

Sometimes nothing is something.

I will nap on tall grass
and roll down distant hills,
even if it's alone.

This world is a playground
for the Gods
and if you can't beat em,
join em.

Is this real,
or am I just high
on validation?

2021

Favorite Sweater

Somewhere there's a sleepy town
Where trees are orange
and autumn is forever
Chimneys smoke animals into the sky
and lovers meet halfway in parks
Everyone wears their favorite sweater
and they talk about love
instead of the weather

Detroit, Michigan
2019

Heavenly Shoes

I was an altar boy
Carrying my tiny wooden cross
that my great grandpa made
from black Walnut
Kneeling in the dirt
and praying with worms and roots

Good news,
you can enter Heaven with dirty shoes

The whole world is a church,
but no one understands.

My spirit is bigger
than any four walls
My heart,
too big for my chest

I've got so much to say
but I won't bother

2019

Stay Happy

I was thinking today
how we're all gonna die one day
I was thinking of all the things
that I take for granted
and sometimes,
I forget how blessed I am

I just wanted to say that
if you're ever feeling down
Truly take a moment out of your day
to think of everything that you cherish

Go squeeze someone you love
put your heart and soul into that hug
and don't let go until you both can't breathe

Just smile
never stop smiling
and if you're ever feeling lost
take a chance
If you've got nowhere to go,
any road will get you there

Dance
and sing
Like no one's watching
If you like someone
tell em'

Stay Happy

Laugh at the stupid jokes only you
and your best friend find funny
Laugh until your stomach hurts

And if you never got the chance to say sorry
Apologize

Life's too short to waste time

Be yourself because nobody else can be

And if you want to cry
cry

"Expectation is the root of all heartache"
The best thing to do is to stop thinking
And to just let things happen
And if the world ever makes you feel small
Look up at the stars
and know
someone somewhere is doing
the same

Stay Happy

just because today
might've been a terrible day
doesn't mean tomorrow
won't be the best day of your life
you just have to wake up and get there

We learn from experience
that we never really learn anything
from experience
We never know what's gonna happen
and that's the thing about life

You just have to breathe every moment in
like it's your last
& never look back
& never regret
& always stay happy

Detroit, Michigan
Febuary 5, 2012

Clowns

The clowns are smoking cigarettes
Fixing face paint in pocket mirrors

The bulls are dancing,
preparing for the gate to lift

I'm looking for a place to sit
There's dust in my hair
and dust on my stadium chair
Trash near my feet
From the show last week

Southern boys know how to get high
and I do too

They're good-looking but stupid

Blonde girl in a flannel
with legs for days

What a shame
One smoke before the city

2018

Parque Chalputepec

watching crows communicate
in some park in mexico
im smoking a joint with bugs on my legs
my lighters in the dirt
it seems most of me is in the dirt
nature is intelligent
obviously nature is intelligent

Noted as an important moment
Parque Chalputepec, La Ciudad de Mexico, Mexico
May 2019

Willow tree

i hope i am a willow tree in the next life
a quiet home in your backyard
where you'll look sometimes
and remember
it's all okay

Detroit, Michigan
2019

Ice & Tea

It's been raining for three days
and the plants seem drunk
I love when you can tell that they are happy

If I want to be a better person
I can be

I am happy to exist on Earth

Thank you

Detroit, Michigan
November 30th, 2020

My favorite little seed

Beautiful things are happening
in the depths of your pain.
Even in the shadows of your sadness,
flowers grow.

I always said that she was like a flower to me,
In more than the way
that she radiates beauty
into my world

It was the way that no matter how many times
the world cut her down,
She grows back, just as strong,
and just as beautiful as before.

My favorite little seed

And I remember the time
she told me,
"Maybe we're more like flowers
than we think we are.
Just like the beauty of a flower is intended
within a tiny little seed..
I think soulmates are like that.
Somehow and some way.
Us, and this moment..
It was all intended the second
the universe first exploded
and planted us into existence like little seeds."

I laughed and said,
"Billions of years of cosmic chaos
And it was all just for me to appreciate
the way the sunset reflects into your eyes?
It all seems kind of silly, don't you think?
All these mysteries of the universe and
You are the only thing
that's ever made any sense to me."

My favorite little seed

It's you.
It's always been you.
My favorite little seed.

I like to think that maybe all those stars
and galaxies
and explosions up there..
I like to think its just a fireworks show

A fireworks show in celebration
to those with the courage to look up

Or maybe it's just the light left on
so we don't forget where home is.

Either way, when I'm feeling alone,
I look up at the stars
because...
Because,

maybe you are too.

Detroit, Michigan
December 28, 2015

Sad movie

I watched you walk away
like every sad movie

They say people don't change
but I think people always change.

They say if you spend enough time with someone
you'll eventually know all about them

I think it's the opposite, you know?
if you spend enough time with someone
you'll eventually only learn to know yourself.

You can never really know a person,
because some things cannot be said or shared.

This is why our parents got divorced.
It takes guts to look at yourself.
It's easy to play it cool for awhile and most of us do.

People sacrifice love to avoid their demons.

I'm daydreaming
about how we exist
in more than one place.

Sad movie

I am aware of my surroundings
but lost in my own world.

I've gotta do the dishes.

Take me to the places only you know
Show me the spaces where you've grown

Lost in a sea of my own mistakes,
I've found an island of your embrace

Entire worlds are hiding in you
Dusty shelves and picture frames
Milky Way oceans

There's a radio inside my head
and all these songs sound like you

the music of wind in trees

the world wrote this tune
for me and you

I hope somewhere you are listening

2020

Me, Coleman, and Fernanda

We've been drinking cactus juice
for what seems like weeks now.
The whole world is closed.
The streets are empty but full of life.
We walk tiny paths with tiny cows.
How are my hands so colorful?
It's only been an hour.

The mountains are alive,
clearly the mountains are alive,
they just don't need to say it.

Huachuma!
The Rites of Eluesis,
in the Arkana garden!

The magic cactus whispers,
"I am of the serpents party
and we will dance into the night"

Urubamba, Peru
April 2, 2020

The War is a lie

There's a man that sends a letter
Heartbroken in the war
From a boy who was a dreamer
to a boy that can't sleep no more
But he's found a way to help strangers
close eternal eyes

He'll be the solider
guiding towards the other side

In his room, he sits alone,
but his mind is filled
with the stuff of home

To be that boy again,
on a swing in the yard

They say it's for your freedom
So I'll sacrifice mine
But as I held the hand
Of my friend that died

I knew it was all a lie

2021

Dance with me at the end of the world

Dance with me at the end of the world.
The sky is crashing,
The streets are on fire,
Everyone is going crazy, but..
Not us.

We're just looking at each other,
with that look in our eyes
like
we knew it all along.

Armageddon is our soundtrack,
and the last song is the best.

So grab my hand and
Please die with me

It'll be so beautiful,
I promise.

Detroit, Michigan
March 7, 2015

I'll be

I'll be your Earth
so you'll always be grounded

I'll be your sun
so your heart's always warm

I'll be your sky
so your eyes stay wide
and
I'll be your moon
so theyll always shine bright

Because I only found myself
when I found you

Detroit, Michigan
Jan. 21 2017

My God, I love you

A girl
from a dream
Sitting grey
and cross-legged
near the circle
at Hart Plaza

Looking up She says,
If we only knew what had happened here
and what has happened everywhere

We would discover that we are survivors
Living in a post apocalyptic-world

We are not our stories
but our stories are important

My God, I love you

And my god
I love you
in the peach wave of a cloud
above corn fields
in Michigan
mid October

Memories of sticky pages
from dirty magazines
in the woods
to parting your lips
and legs

She asked,
"If you're happy then why are you so sad?"
I didn't have an answer

I'm not afraid of dying
I think i'm just gonna miss everybody

Detroit, Michigan
August 29th, 2022

Somewhere, under moonlight

Somewhere, under moonlight, she dances
Bare feet, dilated eyes, and flowers in her hair.

She's the perfect combination
between "Whatever" and "I don't care."

She's the kind of person that shakes you up
and turns your world upside down.

It's like you're just watching her, and then
all of a sudden, you remember that you're alive.

You remember that you're alive.

It sounds silly because you wake up every day,
but the days that she's around..

The days that she is around are different.

There's something divine
in the moments shared
with a free spirit.

Somewhere, under moonlight

Days with her just seemed slower, y'know?

You feel like the moment's gonna last forever
so,
you take a look around,
and you notice the beauty
in everything for the first time

From speckled dust floating in sunbeams
to the melody of wind in dancing trees.
The world is filled with beautiful magic,
and she was the one who dared me to look.

Some people are artists
and some people are art.
But, my God,
she's both.

So, wherever you are,
may starlight guide us to each other.
Because somewhere under that same moon,
I'm thinking about you.

Detroit, Michigan
December 20, 2015

She longed for the stars

Part of me thinks that she lost her mind
and another part of me thinks,
maybe she found it.

She always dreamed about running away,
and then one day she just left.

No phone calls to anybody,
no hugs goodbye,
no notes,
nothing.

She longed the stars.
Lifting rocks for something more,
She made friends with trees,
and she'd kiss the moon goodnight.

The irony of how she saw beauty in everything
but herself.

My favorite part about the sunset
is how it reminds me of her.
Everyone could see it,
She's the kind of girl that shines like the sun,
and she has no idea.

She longed for the stars

The entire sky with all its stars and moons
and milky white arms could do it's best
to push her down
but she'd still rise again
the next morning
just as beautiful
as the day before.

I miss her.

and I hope she's smiling
somewhere.

Maybe she found a cliff,
overlooking deathbed rocks
and ocean waves

Ready to tell a story
she never knew how to say

I don't know if she dove head first,
Or if she learned to fly.
Either way,

I hope she found it in herself to float away.

PNW Roadtrip
USA Febuary 12, 2016

Cocaine

I never needed more
but
you needed that boy
who loved you for your nose

i loved it for the freckles
he loved it for the coke

getting high upstairs
from a mattress on the ground
Tv static sound
mouth open
it's 2 pm
and you're still asleep

there's not enough water in the world
to cleanse our hands

who would have thought we'd end up here?

Detroit, Michigan
2017

Something Beautiful

I always loved the idea of us
in the same that the stars are beautiful
from far away.

I've burnt every home I've built in the sky.

There are universes in my head
and i'm getting lost again and again.

I drift through spaces of where you were.

The lights from your stars still shine
but it's long burnt out.

The universe is endless
and thoughts are the same.

A sad constellation with no one around.

Maybe i'll find some far away planet
for me to rest my head
and i'll speak with the flowers
and the moon there
and i'll let them know
about how something beautiful
once happened

Los Angeles, California
2018

My dearest sunflower

I want to be the wind
that sweeps you off your feet
I want to be the melody that you hum
before you fall asleep
The cliff that makes you fall in love
I want to be the wave that pulls you under

Know I don't have much to give,
but I'm hoping my heart is enough.

I told her that she reminded me
of a summer sunflower.
Lovely and beautiful.

She smiled.
Her smile was like the sun to me,
Lighting my world
and in the way I need it to survive.

I miss her even when I'm next to her,
and I love her more with every second.

My dearest sunflower

Forever used to seem like a silly idea to me
before I met her.
But if there's one thing I know now,
Out of all the uncertainty
and out of all the fucked up things in the world,
forever isn't long enough, with her.

But it's the best we have.

So as for forever,
I'll see you there.

Detroit, Michigan
June 13, 2013

in love

Pretty brown eyes
and shoes too big

I will take care of you
Even when you're old
and your bones hurt
or now when you're young
and your bones hurt

There's a warmth in our hearts
Older than our bodies

A forest fire
One tree at a time
Until our thousand
arms burn together

Animals hide
in your little branches
Quiet coyote
Come close
Stay near
For now

in love

When we become ashes
we will grow again
in love

I could lay with you all day,
in beds in Bangkok

Weed and lovers

If it makes us happy
it doesn't have to make any
se
ns
e

Bangkok, Thailand
September 2022

1,000 moons

You are ten thousand moons
Behind the light of the sun

The reaching of moonlight arms
around me

The rush of night wind
on hillsides of wheat and weeds

My smoke breath
Fades effortlessly
like the days of my life

People screaming
People crying
First-time humans
laughing
dying
I am people
and I have grown like grass
from the Earth

like you

1,000 moons

So
If you need me
Look under your bare feet
If you need yourself
Look under your bare feet

Poseidon is reluctant but not dead
There's an ocean
sleeping inside of your mouth
Calm storms
and how they brew

Something is coming one day
We all know it
But pretend not to

You are happening,
Right now
Right this second,
You are happening
and it is beautiful.
Trust me

Detroit, Michigan
November 2022

Old man

One day
I'll be an old man
Orange from some firelight
And i will tell children stories
of magic and madness.

I'll point at the stars
and explain where we come from
and where we will go.

I'll tell them how the whole world
is the back of a turtle's shell.

I'll whisper mysteries
about how the plants are alive
or how we are made of tiny spirits
and empty space that gathered together
in temporary celebration of this very moment.

And someday, not far from now,
I will be the friend who's died

and when I get bored of death

I'll do it all over again

Urubamba, Peru
2020

What can I say?

What words can I say that Kerouac, Watts,
or Whitman has not already mumbled?

They all died anyway
and the world still needs saving

I, too, dream of young Americans,
barefoot in every city.
Zen freaks, all of em'
carrying weird plants
in colorful rucksacks.
Smoking weed,
making love,
stacking rocks

Everywhere they go,
a gleaming trail of human feet prints
left behind them.

They visit holy sites and create new ones.
They will reclaim the Earth as the body of Christ
and make every forest a temple again.

They will walk deserts
and climb mountains for no reason
other than to invoke living beauty
in all moments.
Maybe it'll happen,
maybe it won't,
maybe it already is

2019

Bananas for Ram Dass

Wintertime in Hawaii
At casa Ram Dass
I wonder what you think about
or if you think at all

You are in the Ocean
I am seeing you in slow motion
You have rainbows above you

And I realized God
is real

It's all so simple,
but not really,
but actually

Bananas for Ram Dass

As long as I push anything in the universe away,
I am not free

When Maharajji was asked
how to raise Kundalini energy
he simply said,
"feed people."

I hope you like the bananas
I chopped from the tree in your yard

Maui, Hawaii
December 2018

Room of witches

I'm in a room full of witches
All they do is sit in circles,
get high,
and gossip
in a beam of orange light
from an October moon
that they pretend is different
from the one in June

Catemaco, Mexico
October 8th, 2020

New shirt

I finally got a new shirt
After 6 down and a month in India
I'm wearing the same pair of jeans
And they're all I need

Plus memories of us somewhere closer
but far from here

I am so many people at once
And they come and go

I think of God in everything

So many different noises
Echoing out from some
eternal background of silence
that never changes

I am somehow the same

New Shirt

I am hate, jealousy, anger,
I am compassion, love, and forgiveness
I am a mamas boy
and a brother
too

I am a man that travels
to touch new grass
and to greet new trees

I am small animals drinking
from a stream far far away

I am tiny bears swimming together

I am the smoke of a distant fire

I am the first lotus growing in ancient water

I am twilight colors,
hugging the sky outside your window
and I am hugging you, too

New shirt

If I can learn to love you,
I can love myself

Because deep down,
I am the eternal background of silence
All I need to do is remember when it's loud

It makes no sense, but it does.

Look closely
Everything you see
is happening within you

The world has not yet discovered
that inside and outside
mean the same thing
or nothing at all

But it makes no difference either way

I like being alone
but hate being lonely

New Shirt

It's all in my head

Even my head is in my head

I know this truth
Only sometimes

I'm just happy for this new t-shirt

Guwahati, India
April 2022

Nature is a poem

Nature is a poem
Heartbroken,
sad and happy
forever

Everything is alive and dead

I sit underneath a willow tree
Nighttime is quiet,
and I am quiet

What is the universe?
It craves beautiful things through me
and that itself is beautiful.

Isn't this moment enough?

There is only one imagination
dreaming itself into lovers,
buildings, and traffic jams.
Frogs in ponds, rats in traps,
honey bees on plants.

My eyelids are heavy
She said,
"Be wild in love
in your heart

and you are with me always."

Nature is a poem

together,
happy,
God,
Goddess,
Shiva,
Parvati,
trees,
soil,
sky,
sunrise,
sunset

I feel like Earth is a waiting room
But I can't remember what we're waiting for

Bargaining with God to keep my hair
but it still falls out
Isn't this moment enough?

My grandma is dead
and everyone I love will die

Isn't this moment enough?

Detroit, Michigan
December 3rd, 2022

Sacred Mushroom

Sacred mushroom
Of the land
I hold you gently
In my hand
I cleanse your soul
and you cleanse mine

We walk together
Beyond time

Eternal friends
In a spiral

At the gates
Of divine arrival

Unsuspecting little savior

I'll eat you now
and you'll eat me later

Bilaspur, Chhatisgargh, India
May 15, 2022

May 4, 2022

It is 11:58 in the morning
on May 4th, 2022.
I've been in bed since this time yesterday
Look at this shit we are calling love

Put your hands in the Earth
and remember who you are.
There is a war for your mind and body.
The revolution is in the grass
and in your heart.

Sometimes I see myself through the eyes of people
That do not even see me

Indian Sunset,
the nature of all subjectivity is delusion.
Stop trying to make it what it was
and let it be what it is
I'm sad that things change
and I have trouble accepting
that it will forever change
it
's
oka
y

India
May 4th, 2022

Prayer

Grandfather of the forest
Most walkthrough,
but I've stopped to listen

Sister of the moon
Most are asleep,
but I see your dancing shadow
in the trees.

Mother of the first river
You are the flow
and womb
of all life

Brother of the mountain
Tell me where to go
You are my guiding stone
And a reminder of home

Eagle father,
Eyes of the sky
show us the sacred way
of the winds
So that we may see beyond ourselves

Grandmother soil,
You have grown me.
I feel the love of your patience
in all steps

Tepoztlán, Mexico
November, 8 2020

So strange

You showed me a ghost town
that's been overtaken and covered in sand.

A whirlwind reclamation of the Earth,
somewhere outside Sharjah.

A living room decorated
with the patterns of billionaire old wind.

Doorways half-buried
and forgotten drawings on the wall.
A cemetery for furniture,
where couches go to die.

Dust shimmers against sunbeams,
diamond Cobwebbed corners
reflecting an equally ancient pattern
.
The world is more dust than a world.
Even the sand knows its fate

So strange

We are temporarily awakened specks

Spellbound by sunsets,
kissing in abandoned mosques,
Holding hands,
Angels in the clouds,
Bugs and birds,
Drunk on blood wine,
high on dirt

It's all so strange

Forgive me, God

Al Madam, United Arab Emirates
November 2021

5:01 am

She feels like a minute past 5 am
Quiet cold and still
Scratching head yawns

Earth
waking up

Arms pulling me warm body close
Tree branches wag whistles and songs
Black and blue bruise clearing infinite

Safe here for now

I will stay awhile

Detroit, Michigan
2022

Maria Sabina

Dear Maria,
I looked for where you've been
Maybe there's something left
I'm sitting in your garden
Soft singing
Sad and tired
I am a tree in a big town
and my body is full of tiny spirits.
I am a tree of tiny spirits.
I am in the place where the Earth speaks
Greenness and sap
there are flowers where you were
And there is clean water
Growing flower of the mountain
I am an echo of your hills
Cross-star woman
Woman who glows in the dark
clown-woman
beneath the ocean
Whirling-woman-of-colors
Big town woman
You are still here,
it seems.

Huautla de Jiménez, Mexico
April 2019

Thinking of Selena

Sneaking weed from an Apple in my room
Eatin' tangerines
Thinking of Selena
Singing sad songs to an empty room
Stuck in the Peruvian quarantine

Mountain man
Star man
River man

The curanderos don't like me smoking so much
It clouds my 'Mimosa Moksha'

Who knows?

I slurp back their sludge of dirt and Earth,
and spirits dance into me

Fancy shoes
and foul sorcery,
to folks back home

Chakruna said,
"Don't take colors for granted, boy!"
And I haven't since that day

Urubamba, Peru
April 14, 2020

I'm in India reading Walt Whitman

Barefoot in Assam

Lonely rice field cow,
leaves of grass,
Earth in my hands,
Women hanging colors on a line to dry

If I could stop this moment for only a second
I could possess the origin of all poems
I could possess the mystery
that suspends the moon
and entangles the planets to stars

How can I then assume the role of my sadness
or my happiness
or whatever fleeting impulse
is blowing in my wind?

I'm in India reading Walt Whitman

I doubt myself in nearly all moments
except when I'm in love.

From here on out, I hereby declare
"I'm in love, I'm in love!"

Am I not equally my breath as I am the air?

Am I not somehow the ground beneath my feet?

Is my flowing blood not somehow
a function of the spin of the Earth?

Is my body not dirt somehow?

Is the Earth not inherent to the space around it?
Does a bee exist without rain?

Today I dance with natures darlings
and tonight too.

Because I knew it poetry.

How can I hold this?

Mayong, Assam, India
May 2022

Boys and girls in basements

What do you think about
when you think about dying?

I think about how I want to hug people

I think about boys and girls in basements
Somewhere outside Detroit
Talking about all the things
And changing

And how they will all find themselves
sitting under a grey sky
some day, sad
because everything is different
But nothing ever changes

Dear God, I love you
But I don't even know who you are anymore

The fact I gotta go
Means I'm already kinda gone

Every second away from the people I love
Is a second I will never get back
Yet I waste time effortlessly

Boys and girls in basements

Life is weird, I'm sorry

I pushed you in a wheelbarrow
through the trail behind your house

I don't actually know anything for sure but
I know that I love myself
when you are around

Detroit, Michigan
Dcember 2022

Dirty Nails

Waist-high grass
and waist-high jeans
You look great
In that old shirt,
tucked in the front

I'm lying on my back
3 pm lovers,
July in the woods

She's an angel with bad tattoos
I told her to dance and sing when I die

She put her hands around my neck
And laughed dementedly

Dirty Nails

Cicada orchestra
Old man coyote,
watching from a bush
Twigs in his beard
Dirt in my nails

How do i fit all this love for you
into my tiny little heart?

The fact that love once happened
means it is somewhere
echoing into eternity,

I think
I hope

God took a breath
and there you were

I am cramming it in

Palenque, Mexico
January 12, 2022

Belladonna

Magic tree
and the dream flower.
Elvish crowns
droop double down silk linens
to spiked stems
Don't let her put it in your tea
or she'll have you for days

November 2021

Detroit 2010

Rusted brown roots of metal trees
creeping from cracked concrete

Dylan and I
in grey marijuana fog
Locomotive lungs
Laughing, hiding being high

Bums by the water
like bears in a campground
Abandoned factory forest

Old haggy tattered ragged woman
Pushing a shopping cart with nothing in it
Somehow symbolic
'The American Dream' for sleepy people
Hopeless-horizon-people
Over-worked-treadmill-people
Shiny-thinged-men
In every battle, the eyes are conquered first
Hypnotized by shine, wearing suits.

If only you knew.

If it seems meaningless, it probably is
but that's not a bad thing
cause the sound of rain needs no translation

On a plane to Cairo, Egypt
November 7, 2021

She grabbed me by the hand and said,
"your head is in your mind.
call it biology or call it magic"

I love loving you

2018

Vagabonds

Her notebook had the words,

"love is only love
when you want nothing from the world"

scribbled onto it

next to tiny blue penned hearts and daisies.

She was dark in a colorful and innocent way.

She once asked me, with a straight face,
to guess which flowers
I think will grow out of my body once I die.

Vagabond queen.
The seat next to her
on a bus going anywhere
is my throne
and all the land is our land.

We owned nothing and we wanted nothing.
We already held the entire Earth
in between the palms of our hands.

Vagabonds

Every moment with her
is as if nothing happens by accident
and that the whole world was planned.

Each intricate little moment implied
when the universe decided to get itself rollin'.

How is it that all the steps I've taken in life
and all the steps these people have taken
and every ancestor breath
or exploding star along the way
lead to this moment?

Falling in love with her
was like a religious experience.

She had a way of making everything feel holy
and the first time we kissed
I found the space behind thought.

Who knows?

It's bigger than we are.

Detroit, Michigan
December, 2022

One day

One day I will rot
with all this love I've got

And flowers will grow
from my little plot

I'm blessed be a garden
But sad to be a pot

Somewhere, Mexico
January 23, 2022

Here's to it

Here's to a life of making a virtue
out of restlessness.

The real revolution is inward silence
expressed in outward dancing.

I am Nataraja,
skipping over fiery American streets

I am what happened here 300 years ago

What's on the news in Afghanistan tonight?

Nobody knows nothin'
and nothin' ever changes
despite how different every day is.

Don't ya know that God is a jazz musician
on a street corner during the end of the world?

Here's to it

I'm homeless not because
I have no ambitions or have given up.

But because home is not a place,
but a quality of being.

A nest of dust on Mars,
a crown of thorns around the heart of hearts,
naked old woman stretching in an ancient cave.

Jesus made his home on the cross
because he was with the father either way.

Wherever I am, the universe is there,
holding me to the ground
and saying hello in happy wind
or sad passing faces on human roads.

I ain't worried
cause we all go to Heaven
in the end

2021

Huachuma

I slurp a cup of cactus sludge
and listen to girls gossip on the lawn

We drink Huachuma every day
and lay in the grass

You won't know you're a tree until you're dead

There's a little cat
and yellow elf crowns
dripping from giant green tree hands

I take a nap with Toé

The shamans said
there's an anaconda living in the river
and it gets angry when we make a lot of noise

There's something to this silence *thing*.

Urubamba, Peru
May 12, 2020

A little piece of you

I put your ashes in the river
Near the woods out by our house
Every step into the water
pushed you further out

Now you're in the atmosphere,
Somewhere way up high
and you'll fall back to Earth
to visit from time to time

You'll say hello through flowers
or from rains drops on the lawn

You'll sing songs through the wind
To let me know that you're not gone

I'll find you in the forest and
On mountain tops too

Everywhere I look,
there's a little
piece of you

Urubamba, Peru
April 2020

Back of a turtle

In a godless age,
people will find a savior in anything

I look over at people wearing hats by the water.

There was something about the birds
and their swaying geometry
and the way this tree fell over
and new trees are growing out of it.

I don't know why
but I asked God to forgive me.

I never meant to hurt anyone
in between my stumbling feet
and fumbling words.

In a way, it feels as if
the human experience has contractual
heartbreak written into it.

I began to tear up,
looking at the ground.

Back of a turtle

God groaned and moaned
and rolled thunder in the distance as if to say
"Why are you bothering me? Forgive yourself."

I've been begging for rain
instead of watering my flowers.

There's something nice in knowing
everything only happens once.
How can anyone tell me my steps are not divine?

My pride is a skeleton.
My sadness is too.

I am blessed by my own illumination.

You paused for a minute as if to
acknowledge the mystery of the moment
but all you said was,
"which jacket should I wear?"

It's all the back of a turtles shell, anyway

Chiapas, Mexico
November 2021

Who can say?

Who can say what this world is?

It all becomes fiction
as soon as we try to speak about it.

Whatever you think it is,
it isn't.

We do not see this place for what it is,
we see it for what we are.

The contents of our thoughts
and the collection of our past experiences
set the stage for us to act out our lives.

It's all just a theatre of traveling souls.

None of it is fully real.
It's all temporary
and anything temporary
cannot be the full truth.

Who can say?

Reality must remain real.
It does not come with names and shapes,
these things are expressions of the mind
trying to make sense of itself.

That which underlies our thoughts
and our experiences
seems to be the most real thing
I can comprehend.

There is a background of silence
from which all sound emerges.

The quiet place where we all come from
and where we all will return.

We are actually there now,

but we are too distracted
by ourselves.

2020

Miss Lara

She picked me up
In a folded hood old thing
That she used to smash a police car
During the Egyptian revolution in 2013

I overslept in a nest outside of Cairo
The down-below bustle of Heliopolis,
yelling in the marketplace
I'm smoking hash
from the balcony on the 3rd floor.

Boney knees and tired afternoons
We've spent a few days together

It's Halloween.
We're looking for ghosts
in old homes
and we didn't even kiss

Cairo, Egypt
October 31, 2017

Neem tree baba

I proclaim my place in the universe,
next to this ol' Neem tree.
Skinny Buddha wannabe
with bees flying around on my yellow shirt.

I put my hands in the grass
and it was like I was touching
the entire world at once.

Nature reclaims everything
It's all food for something

Even the Earth will become food
for some billion-year-old mystery

It is all my home

Sudzal, Mexico
December 2020

(Ariel Leome, praying under our self-proclaimed sacred Neem tree after a Sapo ceremony. April 23, 2021 Sudzal, Mexico)

Blues, stars, and the moon

I'm sick of writing
about my blues, stars and the moon
but what else can I say?

An ode to every person
who's ever watched a sunrise
since the beginning a time

It is my time to cry as the human spirit

My name is every human being
that has ever lived

I am the men who walked
with the intention to burn villages
I am the children and women afraid
I am the blood on the ground
and the grass it fed

Blues, stars, and the moon

I have been a stranger on a bus
i've been Shiva in eternal dhyan
and Jesus weeping from the cross
I am the first and last flower

How can I not be?
Are you not the same?

Is what makes me alive,
not the same in you, and in everything?

Do not be hypnotized
by the story of your current life

Something in you is bigger
and you know it

2022

Dandelion Dharma

I am hopeless,
listening to birds
Moon crazies,
freaks, and trees

If I had a soul,
I sold it for pretty girls,
a pretty world
and a couple of joints

The angels roll their eyes at me
and I roll mine back

sunflower sangha, strange little saints,
quiet
and colorful

"The trees are Buddha's, don't ya know!?",
I proclaim to a group of cross-legged Church girls

"There was a bougainvillea tree that some dogs
chewed completely.
Its dead flowers are still around
and they blew in the wind.
It sounded like tiny footsteps
running towards me."

Dandelion Dharma

I look at strangers and
dream about how my life could be.
The whole world is going and going
with nowhere to be.

Background faces,
obeying street signs,
strolling through time to inevitable death,
eating ice cream

This dream catcher hasn't caught a damn thing yet.

Another day on Earth
From Eden to my room
A child of time,
Waiting for my turn at infinity

The barrier between worlds
is a breath away

Urubamba, Peru

April 9th, 2020

Temple of collapsed stars

I love you in a way
no arrangement of sound could capture.

You are a temple of collapsed stars.

A barefoot constellation,
dancing your way through wild flowers.

You have a soul that flows like water,
soft and gentle or strong and overcoming.

You have a redwood heart that keeps beating
forest fire after forest fire.

I found you in a place
where your feet dangled from crescent shadows
in the sky

and the tides of your breath
pulled me in

Detroit, Michigan
April 2016

Quiet moon

I will love you in the quiet moon.
A cold color-bruised sky and
I am just water in your shaking hands,
the safest place to lay my messy head.

Your heart beats in time with ocean tides
and,
I am drowning in the depths of my mind.

I am coming up for air
to realize you were my lungs all along.

You were my lungs all along.

October 6, 2018

Grass

The grass is green somewhere
But it's dead where I am

I follow my feet
To orphans in the street
and cows in the marketplace

These are the good ol' days
I just don't know it yet

A sparkled glass diamond trail
to a temple no one visits
Watch where you're walking
but keep your head up.

New Delhi, India
2019

Stuff

If we were created from exploding stars
then that means we are equally the stuff
that made the stars
and equally the stuff
that made that stuff
all the way back
to the first stuff.

ALL STUFF IS INSIDE US

There is an eternal silence
that strings it's way
throughout all stuff.

It has been going on forever
and will continue to go on forever.

While we are busy, and planets are spinning,
the eternal womb of stuff
pays no attention to any of it.

It has seen it all before.
Things come and they go.
Just like thoughts.

2021

Noise

We arise from the noise
The whole universe was speckled
in an old fashion
black and white television dots,
until you smack the side of it.

all of a sudden, planets with trees a
nd people show up.
Jazz music,
gas chambers,
and lovers in parks.

There's noise in the street
and in my mind.

Noise

Noise, noise everywhere.
Everything is made of noise.
Vibrations, waving through time.

This fan is spinning so quick
it almost seems solid.
I guess it is solid if it spins fast enough.
The world is spinning fast, too

when I'm in love, I get the strength
to drag my feet in the dirt
and slow this baby down enough to feel alive.

Because for whatever reason,
I am alive, so I better listen while it's here.

Noise

2021

Blu of Earth

Mango meat in her teeth
and leaves as big as her head

She is full of what the sky is full of

Across the room feels like oceans
and I'd lay my jacket over the cosmic waters
for her

Sometimes medicine means
just being around the right people

Sudzal, Mexico
December 2020

Magicians Pot

shaman sludge
magicians pot
mix it with your tears
and drink it up
the ugliness within you is beautiful
memories replaying in a carnival mirror,
spinning in infinity
peyote gods,
in the mud,
baptism by fire.

Sudzal, Mexico
December 2020

Carolyn Jean

A burning cigarette
nestled between your fingers
Forgotten coffee in the microwave
And on the counter too

Doberman-darling
Sci-fi honey
Red-polish-baby

I'm playing hooky
Just to eat breakfast with you

Trying to smoke you out, but you won't

Tell me those same stories of ghosts and gossip

You kept the whole world safe
Life with you was not long enough

But it's weird cause I can still hear your voice
I know you well enough to close my eyes
and say hello

Losing you was like losing a limb

Carolyn Jean

I got high in the jungle
and had visions of you
as a young woman,
in love
Reliving your favorite moments
In eternity

So
until my turn comes
and I can relive some of mine
I am thinking of you

Nov. 2021

This is the afterlife

I have died a million times
and I will die again tomorrow

I have become wood and fire and
ashes are not the end

This is the afterlife, don't ya know?
Form comes from the formless
and formless comes from the form

Just like the moon reflects
into a thousand rivers at once,
the soul hides, untouched, in all things

A laughing Buddha is pointing at me,
and I'm pointing at the moon

My life is a cosmic joke
But it's beautiful

This is the afterlife

The soil and the tree are the same thing
The bees and flowers, too

Whatever this world is,
it exists only in relationships

The poets are the words
the words are the pen
and
the pen is the paper

Inside and outside mean the same thing
Or nothing at all

Urubamba, Peru
April 13, 2020

Untitled File

Time seems to go quicker the older I get

If a thought arises, kill it

.

I'm in this ugly raincoat
and I am looking for the Buddha.

The temples want money
and the mountain tops are empty,
except for some plastic trash,
left by the woo-hoos
who carved the path before me.

I write and write and write.
My mind rolls and unfolds
like an endless bulge of highway roads.

I am trying to say what
I mean, but words are clumsy.
In the end, i can't find my point.
I actually can't find a point to anything
but for some reason, here we are

Human beings are natural storytellers.
It's all we know.

Untitled File

The human experience is theatre
and we lose ourselves brilliantly.

The water settles when I shut up.

A weary message from an old man
with shaking hands,
"If you meet the Buddha, kill him."

Silence is better than bullshit

2019

Swimming in Goa

Her skin is like the sand
And she didn't have her top on
My heart was in my trunks
We went swimming
And she held me under water
Like she wanted me to die
But she pulled me up just in time
With her eyes and evil grin
I'll love this girl forever

2022

My Sweet Joni

My sweet Joni,
You'll be leaving soon
Making your way back toward the moon
I remember when we were kids
You were a free bird in Paris
I was lost in the blues
and a case of you
We would cry and we would sing
and i'd watch you strum them ol strings
You'd paint yourself
or the flower shelf
I'd write about the past
and how I hated myself
But i'm better now
and you are too

2018

Bananas

Us eating bananas somewhere pretty
I know we don't really think about it
because it's normal
but sometimes I'll look at an you
and you will be looking back at me
and I'll get thrown into this vastness
and spacious conclusion
of the fact we are both just here,
in some unexplainable mystery
but here we are
just looking at each other,
sharing a moment
of strangeness and bananas

2019

A boys dream

Wrapped around my waist on
a flimsy oak mattress in the middle of woods
I love her skin a copper coil
mosquitos and weird bugs

You are a boys dream

Goa, India
2019

Mahadev

Wanderers do not become Buddhas,
they become poets

Storytellers never reach Nirvana,
but their words'll take you there.

They say when you write a poem
that it's no longer yours
that it hitchhikes itself
from heart to heart in whomever it meets.

i'm not sure who these words are about.
Sometimes words just want to be alive
for the sake of whoever needs to hear them.

Jesus grabbed me by the hand
and carried me through Buddha's empty land.

Shiva danced around my corpse,
1,000 heads with crowns of thorns.

Krishna's form is all of time,
and he's come to engage
and take my mind.

2021

Coyotita

Jasmine rubbed dirt on my forehead
before she'd let me walk into the forest
near her home.
She took me to some white cross
to leave corn as an offering.
She really means it and
I don't believe in anything.
But I want to.

A girl singing to boys in the forest
playing in mud

She looks like her mom in this light
and she's heard that before.

People don't understand how beautiful they are

I listen to her hum while she burns copal
Healer of hearts

Coyotita

This dirt grew me
even though I'm miles from home.

Cell phone torches light some old
Zapotec pyramid that a farmer found
while digging on his land.
He's hiding it from the government
but Jasmin showed us anyway

There's an Eagle in my head tonight

Oaxaca, Mexico
September 30th, 2020

Oaxaca

I bought a peyote button
from a market in Oaxaca
and now it lives on my lap
in a bus to Catemaco.

I watch a bird die on a beautiful beach.
Life is gravy.
She's been trying to get me naked
since we met a year ago.
I don't fall for it
but I probably will eventually.

Somwhere, Mexico
2019

Our pile of dirt

It's hard to leave
until you do
and then you wonder
why you stayed for so long

The road outside my house
leads to the whole world.

Stars bend above the tree in my yard
and every place is the right place
when you've got nowhere to be

Pick a direction
cause they're not real anyway

Our pile of dirt

I will walk through this life
falling from the sky

I chase adventure
like i've chased women.
Holy men and weird plants
have come and gone.

Throughout it,
the only spirituality I've found
is the same ol' spirit
I've carried with me all along

and what I've discovered,
out there in the world,
is that there's nothing better
than sitting in a big pile of dirt
with someone you love.

October 2021

Perfection in imperfection

Nobody is perfect
until you fall in love with them
Perfection is found in imperfection
and anyone that's been in love
knows what i'm talking about

It's the quirks that become
unbearable to live without

How you carry salt in your purse
or your constant craving for carrot juice

Perfection isn't in Heaven
It's right here, right now

You just don't notice until it's gone

She taught me that
you can spend a lifetime waiting on Heaven
or simply focus on love and realize
you're already there.

Detroit, Michigan
2022

Is there a difference?

Are we just noise vibrating out
from a cosmic explosion
that was so powerful
the echo became dense enough
to create what appears as solid matter?

Are we the boredom of time?
Are we spirits?
Is this the afterlife?
Are we the great imagination losing itself?
Are we in a virtual predicament?
Is there a difference?

Detroit, Michigan
December 2, 2020

I've been

I've been down the dirt roads of Urubamba
and behind the Taj Mahal
I've sat inside a circle of gypsy witches in Romania
I've climbed the Great Pyramids of Giza
I've spoken with holy children of Oaxaca
Drank plant potions in the Amazon
Gotten naked with the Naga of India
I've kissed pretty girls
in the empty baseballs fields of Detroit
I rolled down the hill billy hills of West Virginia
I got high in Kingston with the Marleys
I've taken acid at Petra
and kissed the feet of a biblical God
I've held the shells of bombs in Palestine,
made in Jamestown, P.A. USA
I smoked a joint of Guarumbo with the Lacandon
and toad venom with the Seri of Sonora
I survived the ping pong shows of Bangkok

I've been

But all I think about is how
I left my heart in Sharjah
And how Dubai was lame

Every road leads home

"All land is Varanasi
All water is the Ganga"

Gods gonna turn me to dirt
and I don't care

The whole world is in my backpack
for now

In the name of the father
and Holy Spirit
Jai Ma

Chiapas, Mexico
October 2022

Mom

Mom
the first mother,
black woman,
the shadow behind the sun,
the darkness after time,
big planet belly,
where I've grown like a ceiba,
sacred tree,
and my roots reach to hell,
and my branch arms hug the sky
and my body durable
and my soul impenetrable

You've given me everything
for nothing

you have one million arms
and see through every eye
you are the filling of every lung
and the lifting of every chest
the beating of every heart

Mom

You are the bubbling
of primordial waters,
when you were young.
Sacred virgin,
Shakti
Tonanzin, Guadalupe,
Pachamama,
Maria, Anita,
Ma Bhavani,
The original womb,
You are the Earth
and the space between
Every word is your name

How can I thank you?
Even when I'm lost,
You are patient.
My human arms are not
big enough to hug you

So every step will be a kiss
every rain drop penetrating
graves and turning death to flowers

Mom

Every autumn leaf crunch
Every crisp winter morning
In the sniffling grey of Detroit
In a divine flower pot of snow
Or whatever.

It's all a reminder that you are here
and that you are real
And when I see you,
I see you in everything
And loving myself is loving you

The queen of hearts

We are together forever
Yours always,

Lacanja, Chiapas
October 13, 2022

Downriver Blues

Nodded out parents
Holes in ceiling
Yellow white walls
Dishes in the sink
Mattress on the ground
Ash stained carpet
Empty pop cans and trash
We do what we can
But mostly what we want
No one cares
Downriver is fucked
And so are we
I can't save my sister
I've tried
Dead friends
Dead moms
And dads that don't care
It'll be okay
Even when it's not
Because we have no choice
but to be okay
even when it's not

Detroit, Michigan
Nov. 16, 2022

Dead flowers

I gave you love like dead flowers.
I've kept every kiss you've ever given me
like unwatered potential
Tucked in between the pages of some old journal.

Maybe we will cross paths again someday

I'll rip out the overgrown grass
So the world can read our names
and some random date of
when we met and when we left

Detroit, Michigan
2016

The universe happens

All of a sudden
the universe happens,
a star explodes,
a place appears
and somewhere in the middle
nothing turns into something
and little people wake up
and look at each other

This is impossible
Yet when I see you
I know this is possible.

I recognize the mystery of myself
and the mystery of how all this happened
and we are just sitting here laughing
and for me,
this is all i need

i don't need to be whole or perfect

The irony of how surrender
allows you to receive loving you

Detroit, Michigan
Dec. 3, 2022

Swamp guts

Swamp guts
Rainbow snot &
Flower breath

There is a tree house in my heart,
where small animals sleep at night

Put your hands in the dirt of me
I want to be somewhere
only you have been

Deep down,
where worms are friends
and ants sip wine

Tiny bears
sitting around a fire
in me

Iquitos, Peru
January 2020

Of all the lives

Of all the lives
you could have walked into,
you walked into mine
and me to yours

Thank you to the stars
that exploded for us to exist

A billion years of tragedy,
unfolding into me and you

I can't believe it's real and maybe it isn't.

Consciousness is the basis of reality.
Consciousness exists to perceive.
Beauty is the perception it desires.
Love is its spontaneous reaction to beauty.

Everything is beautiful
and I am in love.

2022

Arunachala

She said,
"In my dreams, you are inside of me"

I laughed because it didn't come out right
But I knew what she meant; I think
Because I feel it too
She is in my heart and head

Plus we wear the same size jeans
and she's got style
it's convenient

Pink clouds over Arunachala
and sad dogs on the street.

I'm writing you from a million miles away
under a million dangling shoestring stars.

"I spring from the pages into your arms.
Do not forget me."

Somewhere India
2019

You Are My Quiet Forest

I want you in the blue-black of a quiet forest.
I want your quiet moon and starry eyes.
I want you in a way
only a trainwreck would understand.
It'll be so sad.
But sad has always been our idea of beautiful.

I want to be the paramedics
that find us lying there together
and if I lose you along the way,
I promise,

Oh my god,

I promise.

I will use my afterlife to
search for you desperately

You Are My Quiet Forest

I'll come back as a firefly.
So, on a lonely summer night,
when your incompleteness
grows like a flower,
and you're ready to give up
We'll find each other again
and you won't

I'll land gently into your hand like I used to.
To remind you that,
"Hey, the world's beautiful sometimes"
I will help you shine,
and you'll hold me like the universe
was made for us
to have that moment.

You won't know why when it happens,
but you'll remember what it's like to die
with somebody you love.

Detroit, Michigan
2014

Rishikesh

I showed her the ceiling
And she pointed to the sky

Rishikesh in monsoon is kinda sad
Bless the rains of India

Discarded plastic blooms
like a million colored lotus flowers

It's just you and me, right, lord?

Girls from Heaven
and cows in the road

Endless Nagchampa alleyways of stuff.
Stuff stacked on top of more stuff.

The sounds of people screaming
in their hotel rooms
as they turn 25 or 30, or 50
or whatever sad year
they've found themselves in.

Rishikesh

Lots of fruit, pretty girls,
pretty sunsets, black magick,
and cool looking bugs

All I know is that a sad summer
is better than a sad winter

I feel to myself,
"not all who are lost are lost"

Being alone in this world
is depressing
and terrifying
and even a relief.

The sun is our star
The Earth, our home
God is the whole universe
Not even some human idea
Not even some form
But the very essence of ideas and form,
y'know?

She texted me saying,
"Don't forget to watch the sunset tonight"

Detroit, Mi
March 16, 2022

Nietzsche was wrong

Nietzsche was wrong
God is alive

God is the wind that blows seeds
God is dirt and a forest of life
and so am I

God is ancient temples in india
and the Muslims putting mosques
on top of them

God is the space between planets
And the forces smashing into them

You don't see God anywhere
if you don't see God in everything

Nietzsche was wrong

God does not only
talk with
Desert prophets
Or dictators
scitzos
and junkies

God is the
seeking and the sought

Bad days
And bombs
Rich kids and
orphans
Sand and sea

You and me

and I ain't really even interested in
enlightenment and all that.

I just wanna sit and wonder
about who I am sometimes.

Chiapas, Mexico
October 2022

Forest People

The forest people are my people
little quiet people,
living in hollowed tree homes

Whisper soft rain into my mouth
Whisper quiet animals
into the rain of my mouth
And forests for them to hide

Dirt piles in my lungs
where flowers grow

Clouds block the sun
and I have visions of people
all around Earth
living at once.

And visions of all people
that have walked where I've walked
or will walk.

Some part of me is with them
And they have no idea

It feels so weird to know I have to die
and that everything is always dying

Forest People

How can I stop myself
from holding on to every second with you?

We fell asleep in a field.
The sky goes on forever
And my thoughts do too

No one says a word
of how strange all of this is.

I like you more than everything

It'll be okay

Jorhat, India
April 29, 2022

Be Here Now

Ram Dass told me to "Be here now."

I think to myself, "where else can I be?"
As my thoughts wander off

I spent a week in Maui chopping down bananas
from a tree in his garden.

He's dead now, and I miss him

and I left her in California
and for some reason
I'm not sad about it.

The sun is shining.
I'm watching the tv,
and it's all bad news.

Be Here Now

I'm having mystical visions
from a couch in Hawaii.

"Shanti shanti"
from a guy panicking with flowers in his hair.

Everything seems ironic.

I don't understand how being alive is real.
What is this?

Which planet is making me sad this month?

No one cares about anything
but is offended by everything.

I've got daddy issues with the founding fathers.

We look for trouble
more than we look for ourselves.

Why should I make my bed
if it's just gonna get messy again?

Maui, Hawaii
December 2019

Slime and angels

Our lives flow
in the triumph
of spirit over matter

We are alive,
inside of organic materials,
temporarily gathered together
somewhere between slime and angels

We all become poets when we are in love
or on mountain tops

And I can fall in love
up to a million times some days

Easy

2021

Space is a cemetery

Space is a cemetery
Where everything is alive
and we are in the afterlife
of stars

The sun is an egg
that'll hatch into a billion people

And those people will play music
and pick flowers
they will become lovers,
they will dance around fires,
eat strange plants,
and paint on rocks

and some moon with its big bald head
and pinhole friends
will be there for it all

Urubamba, Peru
April 22, 2020

Barefoot like the Earth

I built a fort in the forest
near the stream inside my mind
We climb creaky wooden steps
to the top of our tree

I imagine every way to think of you.

a little girl swinging from a tire,
with grass-stained blue jeans,
scraped elbows,
and dandelions stuffed
into her pockets

Somewhere, sad, lonely,
ready to give up,
but you don't.

On a porch, years from now,
barefoot like the Earth,
sitting with someone you love,
looking at them with the same
ol' eyes you looked at me with

An old woman with dirty hands
and denim overalls
planting tomatoes in her garden

Barefoot like the Earth

How do I love you?
Let me count the ways.

If only you could see into me
and see what I see in you

You are not your body,
temporary and delicate
You are filled with fields of deer and dew
You are time itself unfolding into a dream,
The spirit of all things

The love of my life

Detroit, Michigan
December 2nd, 2020

(American poet and traveler Dakota Wint,
in La Venta, México.)

For more information please visit DakotaWint.com
or follow @DakotaWint on social media

and please leave a positive book review online

Thank you for reading

Barefoot Like The Earth

Printed in Great Britain
by Amazon

27108076R00096